THE GEARHEAD'S GUIDE TO
DIRT BIKES

BY LISA J. AMSTUTZ

Raintree is an imprint of Capstone Global Library Limited, a company incorporated in England and Wales having its registered office at 264 Banbury Road, Oxford, OX2 7DY – Registered company number: 6695582

www.raintree.co.uk
myorders@raintree.co.uk

Hardback edition © Capstone Global Library Limited 2023
Paperback edition © Capstone Global Library Limited 2024
The moral rights of the proprietor have been asserted.

All rights reserved. No part of this publication may be reproduced in any form or by any means (including photocopying or storing it in any medium by electronic means and whether or not transiently or incidentally to some other use of this publication) without the written permission of the copyright owner, except in accordance with the provisions of the Copyright, Designs and Patents Act 1988 or under the terms of a licence issued by the Copyright Licensing Agency, 5th Floor, Shackleton House, 4 Battle Bridge Lane, London SE1 2HX (www.cla.co.uk). Applications for the copyright owner's written permission should be addressed to the publisher.

Edited by Erika L Shores
Designed by Heidi Thompson
Original illustrations © Capstone Global Library Limited 2023
Picture research by Jo Miller and Pam Mitsakos
Production by Tori Abraham
Originated by Capstone Global Library Ltd

978 1 3982 4837 3 (hardback)
978 1 3982 4838 0 (paperback)

British Library Cataloguing in Publication Data
A full catalogue record for this book is available from the British Library.

Acknowledgements
We would like to thank the following for permission to reproduce photographs: Alamy: Aflo Co., Ltd., 14, Mette Holm, 6, Tetra Images, LLC, 27; Getty Images: piola666, 21, Thomas Barwick, 23; Shutterstock: Artur Didyk, Cover, 28, Fede Desal, 11, i3alda, throughout, design element Kekyalyaynen, 25, Mariel Camacho Cuba, 13, nattanan726, 5, Pavel1964, 9, Pressmaster, 15, Proshkin Aleksandr, 26, Ronald Plett, 29, Stephen G. Page, 17, Teemu Tretjakov, 18, Tiggy Gallery!, 7

Every effort has been made to contact copyright holders of material reproduced in this book. Any omissions will be rectified in subsequent printings if notice is given to the publisher.

All the internet addresses (URLs) given in this book were valid at the time of going to press. However, due to the dynamic nature of the internet, some addresses may have changed, or sites may have changed or ceased to exist since publication. While the author and publisher regret any inconvenience this may cause readers, no responsibility for any such changes can be accepted by either the author or the publisher.

Contents

READY TO RACE 4

SPEED UP 6

RIDE TOUGH 12

LOOK COOL 26

    GLOSSARY 30

    FIND OUT MORE 31

    INDEX 32

    ABOUT THE AUTHOR 32

SURREY LIBRARIES	
12082675	
Askews & Holts	05-Jul-2023
629.2275 SCI	

Ready to race

Braaaaaaap! Hear those engines rev. Dirt bikes are fast and tough. These small motorbikes tackle dirt, sand and mud.

Want to make your dirt bike even better? Try a few of these tips.

FACT
Riders do jumps and stunts in freestyle events. Judges award points for their performance.

Speed up

Rough trails can slow you down. They can make a bike hard to control. Try a new suspension. It will give you a smoother ride. It can add **traction** too.

FACT
Make sure you wear a helmet, goggles and other safety gear when you ride.

Stock fuel tanks aren't very big. So you may want a larger tank. This helps in a long race. You will not have to refuel as often. It lets you ride further on trails too.

You can also upgrade the **exhaust** system. This gives the bike more power and speed. It will look and sound cool too.

FACT
Motocross, supercross and enduro are different types of dirt bike races.

Sprocket size can affect a bike's speed. Want a higher top speed? Try a bigger front sprocket and smaller rear one. Or maybe you want to speed up faster? Then switch the two.

A **chromoly** sprocket is strong. It is not too heavy. Lighter parts make your bike faster.

You're riding a rough trail. The bike bounces off rocks. The bars twist and jerk. A steering damper can help. It is like an extra pair of shocks. It will help control your bike.

Stock grips can be hard on your hands. They may give you blisters. Try a softer pair. Grips are made of different materials. Some have more "squish" than others.

You might want to try a folding shift lever. It is less likely to bend if you tip over. Add lever wrap too. It will stop your hands from slipping.

A big rock can bash a hole in your engine. A skid plate keeps the engine safe. A wide one will protect the side cover.

You can add brake guards too. They will protect your brake **rotors**.

Choose the right tyres for your bike. Are you riding motocross? Or do you ride trail or desert? Pick the tread pattern and size that fit your needs.

A flat tyre is bad news. Swap your inner tubes for bib mousse. These foam tubes will never go flat. No more blowouts!

Bars come in many colours and shapes. Some can bend. These help prevent **arm pump**. Add a one-piece bar mount too. It will stop bars from twisting if you crash.

Bar ends protect your grips when they hit the ground. Put foam grip donuts on the other end. They will protect your thumbs.

Branches can whip your hands on the trail. A pair of hand guards can help. A metal bar covers your hand. A plastic piece keeps rocks and branches out. It will protect your controls too.

Foot pegs can get worn down. You need a strong grip with sharp teeth. Your boot should lock in place. **Aluminium** pegs are light and give lots of traction. Add a foot peg cover too. It stops mud from getting stuck under the peg.

FACT
The longest motorcycle ramp jump was in 2008. Robbie Maddison jumped 107 metres (351 feet).

Look cool

A bike's plastic cover can fade and break over time. Get new plastics if they are in bad shape. Good ones will stand up to wear and tear.

You can also make old parts look better. Rub faded spots with sandpaper. Wipe them clean with soap and water. Then heat with a hair dryer.

Does your bike need a fresh look? Add some graphics. Rim **decals** can bring a splash of colour to your wheels. Other decals jazz up your fenders and forks.

With these hacks your dirt bike will look and run better than ever. Now you're ready to hit the track!

aluminium lightweight metal

arm pump pain in the forearms

chromoly mixture of two metals called chromium and molybdenum

decal design printed on a sticker

exhaust pipes that carry gases away from an engine

rotor disc-shaped part of a brake assembly

sprocket wheel with a rim of tooth-like points that fit into the holes of a chain

stock parts of a vehicle installed by the factory

traction amount of grip one surface has while moving over another surface

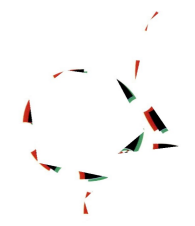

Books

Cars, Trains, Ships and Planes: A Visual Encyclopedia to Every Vehicle, Clive Gifford (DK Children, 2015)

The Tech Behind Off-Road Vehicles (Tech on Wheels), Matt Chandler (Raintree, 2020)

Wheel Sports (Extreme Sport), Michael Hurley (Raintree, 2011)

Websites

www.bbc.co.uk/programmes/b0bpq7rd
Watch this episode of Catie's Amazing Machines about off-road machines.

www.dkfindout.com/uk/transport
Find out more about different types of transport.

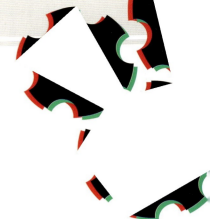

arm pump 20

bar mounts 20
bib mousse 19
brake guards 16
brake rotors 16

decals 28

engines 4, 16
exhaust system 8

foot pegs 24
freestyle 4
fuel tanks 8

grips 14

hand guards 22

plastic covers 26

safety gear 7
shift levers 14
skid plates 16
sprockets 10
steering dampers 12
suspension 6

traction 6, 24
trails 6, 8, 12, 19, 22
types of races 8, 19
tyres 19

About the author

Lisa J. Amstutz is the author of more than 150 books for children. She enjoys reading and writing about science and technology. Lisa lives on a small farm in Ohio, USA, with her family.